A Grandfather's Wisdom On How To Escape Credit Card Debt

A Grandfather's Wisdom On How To Escape Credit Card Debt

Dennis Wragge

ISBN: 978-1-365-91533-8

To my grandchildren –
Jessica, Aidan, Jaxon, Jason,
Regan, Kaden, Christopher, Isla,
Filippo, Michael & Martino

My prayer is that you will
each live a life free from
the burden of debt.
Love Grandpa

Table Of Contents

Introduction

This booklet has been written to enable you to find financial freedom. I have interviewed hundreds of couples over the last decade and after pointing out a few tips and pitfalls about debt, the common response is *"Why didn't someone tell me?"* or *"This should be taught in school"*.

If you are an average Canadian you will be spending close to a million dollars in interest during your lifetime. Most of this money goes through our hands without much thought or daily attention. If left unchecked, the amount we pay can easily double and the system is designed to allow the doubling to take place without us even being aware that it is happening.

The one thing that determines how much we pay in interest is our credit rating. This rating is based upon our spending and payment habits. If you pick up and follow the tips outlined in this book, you will be well on your way to saving hundreds of thousands of dollars. The beauty is that all this money can be yours and you do not need to change your job, work longer hours or do anything to increase your income.

I cannot overstress the importance of getting and keeping a good rating on your credit cards. Everyone needs to have and use three or four cards. There is absolutely no other way to establish a credit history. In the very old days we were taught that we could establish a good credit reputation by paying our electric, telephone or other bills on time. This is not the case today. Paying these bills on time has no effect on your rating. They are not recorded. Neither is a record kept of how we pay our rent, utilities, and donations or how we repay loans from our mother-in-law. On the other hand, every transaction on our credit card is recorded and counted.

Some well-known authors and TV "experts" advise that you cut up all your credit cards and just use cash. As you progress through this book you will find common sense reasons to ignore this advice (Chapter 8.) Everyone needs credit cards. You need one to stay at a hotel, buy on line, rent a car or even rent a tool. I have received applications for a mortgage from people who had no credit cards and therefore no rating. No bank would give them a mortgage.

Without a credit card people lose out on getting interest-free money (Chapter 7) or money back (Chapter 15). Credit cards are necessary. So it is vital to understand exactly how they work and then to use them to your advantage.

I love receiving success letters like the following.

"Dennis, thank you so much for taking the risk with us last year. We have used the last twelve months to improve our credit rating to the point where we can qualify for a new mortgage at the Royal Bank. The savings will be $865.00/month."

David and Amy

"We were not happy when you made us buy the financial book. We thought it was a waste of time but seeing as we spent twenty five dollars we read a little bit at a time and put some of the suggestions into practice. Little by little things began to sink in and we changed our ways. It has taken us three years, but we are beginning to have hope and see light at the end of the tunnel. Thanks, Dennis."

Ken and Sara

"Thank you for the offer to renew our loan to you for another year but we have reached the point where we do not need your help. Maria and I appreciate all you have done for us in giving us the opportunity to improve our credit score. We can now get funding from our bank, which will save us over a thousand dollars a month from what we were paying on cards two years ago. The book was helpful but more so, the education you gave us in the time you spent in our house

letting us in on the secrets of credit card debt. Thanks a million."

Joseph and Maria

I would love to receive a letter like this from you as well once you have achieved your financial freedom or have even started on your journey to escape from debt.

Helping more people find this kind of financial freedom is why I wrote this book. But now you should be asking who I am and why you should listen to me.

Chapter 1

Who Am I and Why Should You Listen to Me?

First, let me tell you who I am and what I do.

I do not think I am particularly smart or wise but I do practice everything I preach in this book. I know what I am talking about. As a person, I strongly dislike injustice and I hate seeing people bound up in debt. It has become a passion of mine to help people get free of the burden of debt.

I have personally known financial hardship. I have known what it is like to miss my mortgage payment. When times were tough, I would walk five miles from north Toronto to downtown Toronto just to save the cost of a subway token. Those days were not pleasant. Today I live in a nice house, which is mortgage free. I can afford to travel the world. Winter vacations are spent in the Caribbean. I ride a motorcycle and drive both a luxury and an exotic sports car, yet I have never earned a large salary or won a lottery. I am embarrassed speaking about myself, but I desire that by sharing my success it will give you hope for your future.

The secret is not how much you make but how much you keep.

It is amazing how much of people's income throughout life is wasted on paying unnecessary interest and bank fees. You can pay nothing or you can pay thousands of dollars each year.

You will find that the tips in this booklet are not difficult to understand or follow. In fact, most of the wisdom contained in these pages I learned from my grandmother and from reading the Holy Bible. Both sources have stood the test of time. Did you know that the Bible is full of tips on how we are to use our money? I have been told that in His parables Jesus spoke more about money than any other subject. I strongly believe that God has a plan to set all of us free and we also have a real enemy who would love to see us in bondage for the rest of our lives. Who you choose to believe and follow is your choice.

What I Do And What You Need To Do

I have a passion to see people get out of debt and in my older years I have found real pleasure helping people do so. My business is simple. I pay off people's debts and give them a breather to improve their credit score. When I work with someone, I do all I can to help but success depends on my clients being committed to doing the heavy lifting.

I help people just like you. Over the years I have sat at many kitchen tables trying to help people get out from under the burden of debt. Many times I have seen middle-aged people crying because of regrets about the life they are living. Financial problems are a heavy burden that can seem impossible to get out from under. Take hope – freedom can be achieved and my desire is that this little book will be your guide to freedom.

If you have impossible debt you are not alone. I have helped truck drivers, doctors, business owners, warehouse personnel, nurses, teachers, executives of major international companies, police, firemen and clergy. The list goes on and on. Anyone can be caught in the trap and no profession or income level is immune.

My business is helping people through refinancing their debt. I used to import a hardcover book on personal finance from the USA. I thought the book was helpful so I required my clients to purchase a copy of the book from me at the discounted price of twenty-five dollars. I was able to sell this book considerably below market price because I bought and imported them in bulk. The reason I did not give the book to my clients was I hoped everyone would value and read the book for their own benefit. My observation had been free books are like pamphlets; they are not treated as valuable.

I think the American book is a very good read. Unfortunately, I do not agree with some of the advice and it does not cover a number of issues unique to Canada.

The American book was thick, hard covered and expensive. It was easy reading with many cute sayings, anecdotes and folksy success stories. I have no regrets requiring people to buy this book, but I began looking for a book written specifically for Canadians. I could not find one, so here is my attempt to put what I think is very valuable information into one small book.

I am not given to many words. In fact, I think a very good motto for life is K.I.S.S., which many will know stands for Keep It Simple Stupid. When you read this book you will notice that it is written basically in short points. There are no fluffy stories, no complicated instructions or formulae to follow. This book could easily have been puffed out to be much longer and more expensive but I have tried to K.I.S.S.

I also had to ask the question – would people find a bigger book intimidating? I concluded the answer is yes. If people are intimidated they will probably not finish the book and that would be a shame. My passion is to help people find freedom, real freedom. This book is informative, not entertaining.

The criteria I look for when helping people is for them to have a strong desire to get out of debt. I will only pay off debt. If people want money to buy more things, go on vacations etc. then they must go elsewhere. My sole purpose in refinancing is to give people breathing room to improve their credit so that within a short time, they can begin their financial life with a clean slate.

I know this book will be of help to anyone already caught in the trap. I also hope it can be used by anyone to prevent them falling into the allure of easy money. I recommend it be given to young people exiting school and any couple contemplating marriage. Our society is geared for failure, and most in the money lending business are skillfully doing all they can to entrap you by their practices and advertising.

Money is useful. We all need it, but I would ask you to remember the words of a wise man in the Bible who did not want to be either rich or poor. He had wisely observed the special problems that the rich have and we all know the effects of poverty. Neither one is desirable.

At this time I would also warn against the love of money. Loving money can become the object of your life and that is a hollow life. My Grandmother used to say, *"Love people, like things."* Wise words! Throughout this book you will see me occasionally quoting both the bible and my grandmother. This is because the wisdom of both has stood the test of time.

Eventually, we will get into ways to improve your credit and the tips you must follow to arrive at financial freedom. But first of all, let's start with an amazing guarantee.

Chapter 2

A Guarantee

This little book could be worth a quarter of a million dollars in real, after tax, Canadian dollars. I know, I know, this sounds like an email offer from Nigeria. But really, I am serious and I hope you will take and use the information contained in this book seriously. Remember, it could be worth a quarter of a million!

I am not going to tell you how to get rich quick. I do not have some miracle scheme that requires you to spend your hard earned money to join in the hope of getting some magical return. Trust me; all those kinds of promises are bunk. Avoid them like the plague.

What you will experience from following the steps outlined in this booklet will change your life, and in half a lifetime (thirty years) it will save you at least a quarter of a million dollars, GUARANTEED, and it will not require you to spend a penny, or change your career; nor will it cramp your lifestyle.

A True Story

To illustrate my point further, let us compare two couples. Both couples have exactly the same income; both own exactly the same cars, house and goods. They have the same lifestyle. Let's call couple number one,

Mr. and Mrs. Contented, and couple number two, Mr. and Mrs. Frustrated.

After thirty years, both the Contenteds and the Frustrateds have paid off their thirty-year mortgages. The only financial difference between the two couples is that it will have cost the Frustrateds a quarter of a million dollars more to maintain the exact same lifestyle that the Contenteds have enjoyed.

The reason for the difference is that Mr. and Mrs. Contented have always had a good credit score and Mr. and Mrs. Frustrated have always had a poor credit score. Because of the poor credit score, the Frustrateds have had to pay a whole lot more for something as useless as bank interest. The purpose of this booklet is to help you be like the Contenteds. You can trust me; the Contenteds' life is so much better.

Why This Book

My first objective is to get your attention, which I hope has happened. Secondly, I want to scare you about the end of the course you are now on. But I'm not just going to scare you; I will educate you about how the system works against you. Then, I will give you tips and advice to help you. Finally, I will encourage you to take the necessary steps to get the guaranteed results.

I am going to spend a lot of time explaining how you got into this mess. I will give tips to help you get out of crippling debt. In the process, I will be saying some nasty things about banks and credit card companies who encourage debt and TV fraudsters who spew out myths and nonsense about personal finances. I will even have a few things to say about financial planners who get rich by giving false advice. (After I've said my piece, I plan to run and hide!)

One strange practice I have is that I enjoy reading legal contracts. I like getting into the fine print on documents. I would encourage everyone to do the same, but I also realize that few will do so. In essence, I am saving you from a task that you probably would not enjoy.

So, hang on. I have a passion and a mission to see you get out of debt so here are a few things I have discovered. Throughout the book you will find many pitfalls you can easily fall into and we will look at some of the ways credit card companies deceive you and steps you can take to avoid the potential traps the banks have set for you. They are out there, but when you are knowledgeable about them, it is your job not to be caught in the traps.

Take Charge

Find out how much money you are spending each year for interest on your mortgage, credit cards, vehicle payments etc. Add in all bank charges on your accounts and at least another $500.00 for extra costs on your car and home insurance.

Chapter 3

Your Beacon Score

What Is A Beacon Score?

We have all heard of a credit score, or more properly your beacon score. This is your life-long credit rating. Every single financial transaction in your life is rated by it. If you have a low beacon score you will be wasting many dollars every single day for the rest of your life. You may be surprised when I tell you that this constant dripping could amount to hundreds of thousands of dollars over your lifetime.

Your beacon score is a constantly changing number assigned to you by a computerized system. Your beacon score goes up or down on a regular basis depending on how you use credit.

I like to envision this system as a massive, faceless monster buried somewhere beneath the northern Canadian Shield. I call it Big Bro. He never sleeps or takes vacations. He is constantly sucking up data and information about every single person and most financial transactions in the country. He then assigns a number to you.

A low beacon score is anything below 650. An acceptable number is above 750. I have seen beacons as low as 410 and as high as 860. This number affects every penny you borrow. Your beacon score is also used by many industries to calculate the price you pay for many of the goods and services you need.

Your credit report is a record of any court judgments, bankruptcies, credit proposals, car leases and loans. It records whom you have asked for credit, all past and current credit cards and your history of payment. It records your past and present home addresses and employment. It even shows your nicknames and pre-marriage names. When a credit card is no longer used, it records if it was cancelled by you or cancelled by the credit card company.

All these transactions are fed into the big computer, which then distills the information down to a number called your beacon score.

Reasons To Care About Your Beacon

If you have a high beacon you can get the best interest rate on your mortgage. You will be offered the lowest rate for your bank loan, your car payment, your car lease, car and house insurance and life insurance. You will get the first choice of an apartment rental. Business people will use it in any transaction where someone is evaluating your character or credit. If you have a low beacon you will <u>always</u> have to pay more.

You will lose out on opportunities. The difference over a lifetime will amount to hundreds of thousands of dollars. Remember, this is after tax money, so multiply your savings by another 43-65% to arrive at the amount of income you would need to make to just be equal.

People always ask why their beacon score affects their insurance premium and here is why. Consider a person who is short on money yet needs new brakes on his car or a new roof on his house. If he is short on funds today, what are the chances he will delay these necessary repairs? If he delays, is he putting himself and his insurer at greater risk?

When it comes to car insurance the government forces companies to insure high-risk drivers, but at a premium rate. If there were an accident, it would be a third party who would suffer loss from an uninsured motorist. This is why you can always get car insurance regardless of your beacon score, provided you pay the higher premium.

Not so home insurance. I know that some insurance companies refuse to insure people with low beacons. This is their right and there are no laws that force them to take on high risks. You quite possibly could not get insurance and you would be on your own. I have seen this happen.

Simply put: if you have a high beacon and you save $10,000.00 in interest in a year, it is exactly the same as a raise in salary of $14,300 - $16,500 per year.

That would be a great pay raise wouldn't it? It is available to you if you take the necessary steps to improve your beacon. The steps are simple and easy to follow.

A Good Living Rule

Never, never, ever spend a penny without thinking about how it will affect your beacon, because big Bro is watching and he never sleeps! Every misstep is seen and recorded.

Always, always be thinking about your beacon score.

Chapter 4

An Old, Old Story

Let me tell you an old, old story.

There was once a shrewd traveller passing through an ancient land. He performed a small deed for the king and upon completion of the task he presented the king with a bill for $2,500.00. The miserly old king objected strongly to paying such an exorbitant amount.

Now the shrewd traveler was very smart and the king was foolish and greedy, so the traveler made an offer the king just could not refuse.

The shrewd traveler said, "Your Highness, I will reduce the debt and I will make it easy for you to pay it off. Here is what I will do. I will reduce the amount you owe from $2,500 to just one cent, but you must not pay me until the end of the month. Since I am such a fine fellow, I will only ask that you pay me interest on the debt.

The interest I will charge you will only be that each day you will double the amount you owe. You will pay me one cent on day one; double it to two cents on day two; double that to four cents on day three; eight cents on day four and so on for the thirty days of the month."

The greedy king was happy to see his debt reduced to only one cent plus interest for only one month.

By the end of the first week, the king was rubbing his hands in glee as he calculated his debt to be only sixty-four cents. By the second week he was still smiling broadly as he calculated that he owed $81.92.

Each day the amount of the debt doubled from the previous day. Then on the thirtieth day the king discovered he owed the shrewd traveler *over five million dollars.*

Do the math yourself.

If the king had to pay one more day, the debt would have been ten million dollars and the day after that, twenty million. That is what compounding debt does. It was too bad for the king that he had not learned the mathematical principle of compounding debt.

How Compounding Interest Affects You

If you only pay the minimum amount on your credit card every month, this same monster will trap you.

When it comes to debt, compounding interest can be your greatest enemy. It is the reason some people never get out of debt. Banks and credit card companies are very aware of the power of compounding. In this book I would like to teach you ways to avoid getting into this trap.

The Golden Rule To Always Remember

Most people can recite the words of Jesus in what is referred to as The Golden Rule: *"Treat others in the same way that you would like to be treated."* These words of Jesus are wisdom and, if followed, would immediately solve the world's problems. Think about it.

Unfortunately, the financial world also has a golden rule, which is true but not so nice: *"He with the gold, makes the rules."* Every banker or lender knows and follows this rule. Always remember this rule when watching advertisements. There is currently a bank running a commercial with the statement, *"You're richer than you think."* They are trying to put you to sleep which is good for them but not for you. Keep your eyes wide open and don't get caught like the greedy king.

Take Charge

From now on watch each advertisement you see and try to spot the deceit. You will notice that every time you save or make money, the ads always try to entice you to spend that and more and take on more debt. For example you are being told, "You're richer than you think" or that you could win the lottery and spend the rest of your life on a yacht or frolicking on a Caribbean beach. That advertisement promises all this if you win $1,000 per week! Stop and think: does an income of $52,000.00 a year give you that kind of lifestyle???

Chapter 5

Three Kinds Of Debt

Debt

Let me be clear, I am not against debt. A modern
society cannot function without debt. You need debt; I
need debt. The important thing to understand is that
there are three kinds of debt. All debt falls into one of
these categories. Let's call them Best Debt, Good Debt,
and Worst Debt.

The Three Kinds Of Debt

Best Debt: Borrow money and never pay the lender
interest. This is free money. As strange as it sounds, it is
possible to legally borrow thousands of dollars from any
bank and never ever pay a penny of interest. More on
how to do this later.

Good Debt: I can only think of three good reasons to
borrow money.
1. To buy a place to live.
2.   To get an education so you can earn more.
3. To begin a business or make a profitable
    investment.

Worst Debt: Here we lump all credit card payments, payday loans etc. I would also include borrowing from family or friends for frivolous spending.

Never, never, ever borrow money to buy stuff or take vacations. If you cannot pay for it today, you simply cannot buy it today, full stop. There can be no exceptions. Wait until you have the money in the bank before you spend a penny. Eventually you have to pay for everything you buy. You can pay for it today and get it over with or you can put it into the worst debt category and be paying for it for years to come. Begin living this way immediately. You may need to change your daily routine, cancel your cable TV or pack your lunch.

Whatever it takes, do not spend what you do not have. It may mean going back to a simpler way of life for a while, but you will survive.

Take Charge

Make a list of all of your debts. Now separate them into Best, Good or Worst Debt. This will give you a goal of getting as much of your debt into the Best category and also a goal of eliminating all your Worst debt.

Chapter 6

Navigating Debt

Best Debt: Borrow Money At Zero Interest

Everybody should have at least three credit cards. Get a credit card that has no annual fee and preferably one which gives you back a percentage of all you spend. Put as many purchases as possible on these cards.

Provided you pay the balance in full by the payment due date, you will never pay any interest. Here is the best part: *it is possible to borrow thousands from the banks and never pay them any interest.* I have legally done this for years. Here is how.

Determine what day your payment cycle begins. Put your large or recurring payments on the card at the beginning of this cycle. Make sure you pay off all charges on the payment due date.

For example, the first charges on my monthly Visa bill begin on the 7th of each month and the payment due date is the 28th day of the following month. I have set up my recurring bills to come out of my account on the 7th day of each month. That means that if I spent $2,000.00 on the 7th day of the month, I pay no interest on this money for almost seven weeks. I do this month after month after month. Free money!

The banks stick it to everyone else – it's beautiful to stick it back to them! Suppose you do this and your expenses are $5000 per month; you have effectively borrowed $5000 continuously at no cost to you. Combine this with getting cash back and you have a sweet deal.

Don't feel badly for the banks. Later on we will look at some of the ways they have been sticking it to you for years and I have never seen a bank losing sleep. The savings to me at their credit card interest rate plus the cash back I get amounts to approximately $2,000 per year. Certainly better in my pocket than theirs!

Good Debt: Borrow For A Good Reason

Most people need a home. Few have enough cash to buy a house or condo outright so the only alternative is to rent or buy. Many experts have different viewpoints about renting but over the long haul, buyers have always come out ahead of renters financially. There are also emotional and tax advantages to owning your home but the financial reasons are that the money goes into an asset, which traditionally appreciates in value. This money is always tax free so, for example, if your home increases $60,000 in ten years, it is the same as an increase in your income of $10,000 per year because the increase is tax free.

Another advantage of owning a home is that you can use the equity in your home to borrow to invest and start a business or use it to pay off high interest loans that you may now have. This can save you a bundle.

Borrowing for an education is also usually a good reason to borrow money. Studies have shown that better educated people obtain better jobs whether to be a plumber, carpenter, real estate agent or lawyer.

Borrow for a business or investment as long as you are sure you will make more than it costs for the funds.

Remember that for all of the good reasons to borrow there is still risk, so be very sure you are buying the right house, education or investment.

Worst Debt: Once In, It Is Hard To Escape

Unfortunately, most readers of this book will have some worst debt. If you have let it get out of control I don't need to tell you how terrible this situation is, or can become. Debt causes stress, disgrace, guilt, and family quarrels. People with debt often fear answering the phone or the door because of bill collectors. I have observed that people with debt often impulse buy, or they are addicted to eating junk food. They justify these harmful actions by convincing themselves that they need a treat to pick themselves up. Some people buy lottery tickets for hope or try drinking for relief. This I call bondage and I hope that by using the tips in this booklet, you will find freedom.

Chapter 7

Five Things Not To Do

Other Things That Affect Your Beacon Score

Of course paying your bills, especially credit card bills, is paramount and something you must do, but paying your bills on time is only one factor that Big Bro sees. He is also watching for trends in your habits and lifestyle. We will now go over some of the things he is watching for and what you should do about it.

Avoid Being Sued

The Bible advises you to make friends quickly with your enemy. If you cannot pay your bill, contact your creditor before he takes you to small claims court. Usually you can make a settlement. All legal actions against you show up on your credit report and they are a huge red flag on your record.

Avoid The Temptation Of Bankruptcy

We are bombarded with advertisements which make the option of getting rid of our debts by bankruptcy seem painless. These people want your money and their promises are alluring, but false.

The stigma of bankruptcy lasts a long time. In fact it can affect you for the rest of your life, long after it stops showing up on your credit report. Some professions are closed to people who have been bankrupt. Also, how would you honestly answer the question, *"Are you now, or have you ever been bankrupt?"* If you have taken the easy way out, you are stuck forever with having to answer yes.

The following are less extreme and probably more overlooked problems that Big Bro sees.

Avoid Shopping For Credit

No one can check your credit rating without your permission. If you check carefully, in every application for credit that you make there will be a paragraph whereby you grant that person or company permission to investigate your credit. Whenever your credit is checked, Big Bro finds out.

Now, if an abnormal number of companies are checking your credit rating and requesting information about your beacon score, Big Bro assumes that you are shopping around for credit and that you must be desperate to borrow money. This may not be true, but how is he supposed to know. He just concludes you are desperate to borrow and are running all over town and having trouble finding someone to lend money to you. Obviously if you are desperate, then you are a greater risk. Therefore he lowers your beacon. Don't shop around needlessly.

It is wise to avoid applying for a credit card that is not necessary. We have all experienced going shopping at a large chain store on Saturday morning and being approached by someone offering an incentive if you apply for a store credit card. I used to think it was harmless to fill out the application, take the incentive and just never use the card.

Not so. The card company will check your credit. Big Bro will notice and assume you are trying to increase your debt. He will bring your beacon down another notch. The next paragraph will explain an even greater problem you will run into with this approach.

Never Cut Up Your Credit Card

A common myth which is put out there in books, by the media and sensational TV shows is that the first thing you should do is to cut up your credit cards. This is very bad advice and here is why.

When you cut up your card, you obviously stop using it. When a credit card is not used, the card company will after a certain number of months cancel your account to free up the number and remove you from their books. Big Bro spots this and on your credit report it shows up as "Cancelled By Visa" or "Cancelled By MasterCard." How do you think a notation like this looks to anyone looking at your report? Their assumption will be, "If these big companies do not trust them and cancelled their credit, I will take the warning and not trust them either."

The only way to safely get rid of an unwanted card is to return it to the card company asking them to cancel the card. The notation on your credit report will now read "Cancelled By Borrower." You have now turned a negative into a big positive. It is a little more work, but it will make it much easier to increase the credit limit on the cards you want to keep.

Take Charge

Return all unused credit cards with a letter asking the company to cancel your card.

Chapter 8

The Biggest Scam Of All

Avoid The Minimum Monthly Payment Scam

So many people fall for this scam that I felt it necessary to devote a whole chapter explaining why it is so bad for you. Banks desperately want you to only pay the minimum every month. After all, they charge you anywhere from 20% to 30% interest! Oh I know, they make it seem like they are doing you a favour and making it easier for you to make your payments by reducing the amount needed to pay your bill this month.

Remember the bad version of the Golden Rule? **He with the gold makes the rule.** Not exactly like the real Golden rule that Jesus taught: Treat others as you would wish to be treated. You can trust the words of Jesus, but watch out for what the banks try to sell you.

On the following pages I have copied the front page and the third page of a typical credit card statement. Please examine Page One of the statement and note the amount I owe under the heading "New Balance". Then check out the large size type "Your Minimum Payment Due." Note the Minimum Payment is repeated over two lines of type. Do you think the larger type and the repetition is to catch my attention? You can bet your bottom dollar that is the purpose and if you think they are doing this for my benefit then please think again.

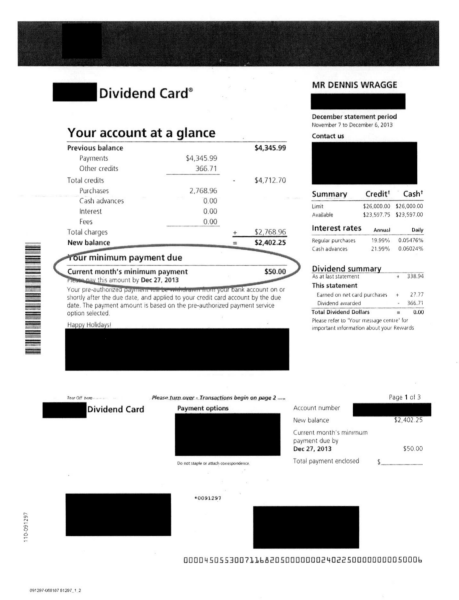

Dividend Card®

MR DENNIS WRAGGE

December statement period
November 7 to December 6, 2013

Contact us

Your account at a glance

Previous balance		$4,345.99
Payments	$4,345.99	
Other credits	366.71	
Total credits		- $4,712.70
Purchases	2,768.96	
Cash advances	0.00	
Interest	0.00	
Fees	0.00	
Total charges		+ $2,768.96
New balance		= $2,402.25

Your minimum payment due

Current month's minimum payment $50.00

Please pay this amount by **Dec 27, 2013**

Your pre-authorized payment will be withdrawn from your bank account on or shortly after the due date, and applied to your credit card account by the due date. The payment amount is based on the pre-authorized payment service option selected.

Happy Holidays!

Summary	Credit†	Cash†
Limit	$26,000.00	$26,000.00
Available	$23,597.75	$23,597.00

Interest rates

	Annual	Daily
Regular purchases	19.99%	0.05476%
Cash advances	21.99%	0.06024%

Dividend summary

As at last statement	+	338.94
This statement		
Earned on net card purchases	+	27.77
Dividend awarded	-	366.71
Total Dividend Dollars	=	0.00

Please refer to 'Your message centre' for important information about your Rewards

---

Tear Off here

Dividend Card

Payment options

Do not staple or attach correspondence.

Please turn over - Transactions begin on page 2 →

Page 1 of 3

Account number	
New balance	$2,402.25
Current month's minimum payment due by **Dec 27, 2013**	$50.00
Total payment enclosed	$_____

*0091297

110-091297

0000450553007116820500000002402250000000000050006

091297-068187 01297_1_2

The first page of my credit card statement shows for that month I owed them $2402.25. When some people receive a bill like this, their immediate reaction is "Yikes – I don't have $2402.25."

But wait – the bank has a wonderful offer to make to you. Note that on the statement, in large and bold print, the bank says that I only have to pay $50.00. Aren't they being nice? NOT!

Now look what's buried in the middle of the third page.

		Amount(S)	Budget (S)	Difference (S)		
Health and Education	5	209.19	-	-	81	5,500.41
Foreign Currency Transactions	0	0.00	-	-	48	3,692.71
Total	29	2,768.96			477	$38,386.99

Transactions are assigned a spend category based on where the goods or services are purchased, not on what was purchased. For example, items purchased at a convenience store in a gas station will appear under Transportation, not Retail and Grocery.

A negative difference (–) means you spent more than you budgeted.

	Amount(S)	Budget (S)	Difference (S)
Total Monthly Budget	2,768.96	-	-

Reminder: If you only make the minimum payment every month, it will take approximately 43 year(s) and 1 month(s) to pay the entire new balance shown on this statement.

Your message centre

No payment required. As you requested, your payment will be withdrawn from your bank account on (or shortly after) the due date. This payment will be applied to your Credit Card Account as of the due date based on the Auto Pay Service Option you selected.

You will notice, in small writing, how long I will be paying the minimum payment. In this case it is 43 years and 1 month! When the bank is collecting interest for that long is it any wonder that the banks want me to take the minimum payment option?

Many people fall for this trap. They don't realize that they will still be paying for the fancy clothes, iPad, or TV they just bought for thirty five years after these goods have been put out to the garbage. Your vacation tan and memories will both fade away, but you will still be paying month after month after month after month...

Easy Solution

Make sure you have the cost of the iPad, TV or clothes in the bank before you buy them. This is especially true of nice vacations. This way you will always have enough to pay your statement in full each month and never need to take the minimum payment option.

Chapter 9

The Hook

Another Terrible Example

Here is another example, and this time I call it credit card evil. I recently received a credit card statement and that month I spent over $7,000. Since I never take the minimum payment option, I guess they wanted to entice me to just try it. The minimum payment option they offered was just $10.00 on a total bill of $7,056.78!

See for yourself.

This was not a fluke or mistake. They really want me to get sucked into the minimum payment scam. I have received other statements with balances in the thousands. Many of them offered a minimum payment option of only $10.00.

All these statements are from the same bank and all on the same account.

Nothing has changed in my circumstances. In my opinion it is just sucker bait – don't ever fall for the minimum payment trap.

Chapter 10

Watch Out!

A Very Nasty Trap

Watch out for this little known fact. Every credit card statement has a payment due date. The bank must receive either the full amount or the minimum payment amount by that date. There are no exceptions.

If you are late, of course, they will accept your money but they will record that you were late. Here is the stickler: if you are late twice in a twelve-month period, your interest rate automatically jumps another 6% on everything you owe. For the next year your interest rate goes up from 20% to 26%. It doesn't matter if your payment was only late by one day.

For a busy family, who are a bit sloppy about paying on time, this little known fact could catch them out permanently if they are late once every six months. Nasty, but true.

It is not hard to imagine a scenario where one spouse leaves a cheque on the kitchen counter to pay the credit card and going out the door in the morning reminds the other spouse to drop the cheque off at the bank. The day becomes hectic and it doesn't happen until the following day. Suppose that happened in May and one of the kids fell in the playground and had to be taken to the doctor. The cheque does not get delivered on time. Then the following February a massive snowstorm closed everything down and the cheque could not be delivered until the next day. Easy to imagine these two events happening in a twelve-month period, but it still cost that family hundreds of dollars. (Not to mention at least two family fights.)

Solution To This Problem

For years I have made the credit card company responsible to take full payment from my bank account on the due date. I have never been late and have never paid interest on any credit card. If the card company did not take their money by the due date, that is their problem, not mine. As an aside, they have never been late to take every penny they are owed.

A Nasty Obstruction To Watch Out For

I recently applied for and obtained a new credit card. I sent them a letter requesting that they set up an automatic payment schedule on my account. The card company sent me back a form letter advising that they did not currently have the facility available to set up automatic payments. Do you believe them? I don't.

When I responded with a letter hinting of my knowledge of the system, they immediately discovered that, oh yes, they actually could facilitate an automatic payment program for me.

Facts To Observe

The facts speak for themselves. The banks do not want you to pay on time. They want you to slip up twice. They want to make an extra 6% on their loan to you and to as many other people as possible. Make sure you are not a victim by setting up an automatic payment plan. My advice is to make the request in writing and do not back down. They do not want to do it, but it is ridiculous for them to claim that they cannot do it.

As long as you do not spend more in a month than you take home in a month you will always have enough money in the bank to pay off your credit card. If you have set up automatic payment you never have to worry about paying your bills on time and you will never pay a penny for interest. Providing you have a card that pays you 1% or more, you will be collecting money **from** the bank and not paying money **to** the bank.

Sweet.

Take Charge

Write a letter to each credit card company asking them to set up an automatic payment plan. Write a separate letter for each account and send them immediately.

Chapter 11

Choosing the Right Credit Limit

Low vs. High Credit Limits

People often think that it is wise to have a low credit limit on their credit card. They assume that a credit limit of $2,000.00 is better than a credit limit of $15,000.00. This common assumption is wrong and here is why.

Let us assume you regularly spend $1,500.00 to $1,800.00 on your credit card. Popular thinking is that it is enough to have a limit of $2,000.00 because you never spend quite that much. Imagine that this $2,000.00 is a ceiling. Every month, when you take your spending up to $1,600 you are bumping close to that ceiling. You may pay it off, but the following month it goes up to $1,800. And, to Big Bro, it looks like you are pushing the limit and bumping into the ceiling. He worries that next month you might go over your limit, which is very bad. He will reduce your beacon score to warn lenders that you are very close to your limit.

The solution to this is to have a limit of $15,000, but still keep your spending at $1,500 to $1,800. Pay off the total amount at the end of the month. Now, you are nowhere near your limit and Big Bro can go back to sleep. Your beacon will start going up as well.

But A Low Credit Limit Will Stop Me From Overspending – NOT

If you are one of those people who cannot control their spending without a limit and believe the lie that "You're richer than you think", then for you the slogan should be "You're dumber than you think." (Sorry about that.)

I have observed that people who use their credit limit as a spending control just go out and get four, five, six cards or more. Every month they bump the ceiling on them all and Big Bro rewards them with the worst beacon score and the banks collect minimum payment interest on each one of the cards.

The next chapter shows one way to help get your spending under control.

Take Charge

Write a letter to your credit card company asking for your credit limit to be increased. It may be wise to wait to do this until after your credit rating has improved.

Chapter 12

Just Too Simple
(But It Works)

Easy Tip For Couples To Control Their Spending

Let me tell you a true story. Many years ago I had dear friends, Ralph and Sandra. They were a young couple with small children who were struggling financially. My wife and I were also a young couple with small children but we were not having a struggle. Ralph had a secure government job but no savings. His salary was more than my salary. I had just started a new job but fortunately I had some small savings.

When Ralph and Sandra confided that they were falling behind, I was able to pay off all their debts. I refused any interest but asked just two things:

1. They pay me back as soon as they possibly could.
2. Ralph and Sandra both had to buy small, spiral notebooks and record every penny they spent and give that week's page to me on Saturday. They also promised to repay as much as possible each Saturday.

The first Saturday, they paid back a small amount. The pages I received from them recorded many small frivolous purchases. I assume they were embarrassed for me to see their foolishness. The next week, there were less frivolous purchases and the payback was larger.

More so the following weeks and the debt was cleared in no time.

I had absolutely no interest in monitoring what they purchased. These little papers were just for their benefit. What actually happened was that they were able to see just how much money they were wasting by buying junk and doing silly things.

I suggest that as a couple you buy two little spiral notebooks, which you carry about all the time. Record every single penny you spend. Pick a night for a weekly date night and exchange your pages for that week.

My suggestion is that you make a joke about your own flaws and mistakes but encourage each other to cut back.

Did I really have to go to Tim Horton's three times? What if we had fun and made a special dinner together rather than eating out? Why did we allow that cheque to bounce and pay the bank $45.00 etc.

Make these dates as much fun as possible. It is very important to work together on this and not be throwing around blame. Please, please don't start a fight!

For those not married, try to get a friend to share. You will both be better off.

Why A Spiral Notebook Is So Important

My grandmother used to say, "You look out for the pennies and the dollars will take care of themselves." Have you ever had a dripping tap or running toilet? What happened? Probably nothing until the water bill arrived and then you panicked. The same happens with your wallet. It is the constant little expenses, and the hidden interest costs which use up most of your money.

In most homes, couples will have a discussion prior to spending larger sums over a certain amount. The greater the amount of money, the more thought is spent and research done to make sure you are buying exactly what you want or need. You are very careful about these purchases. This is not the case with the small purchases where money goes out without any thought. But I can guarantee you it is the small amounts that are killing you.

If you both keep track of these small amounts in your spiral notebooks, I suggest that at the end of the month you tally up the amount of small purchases and I promise you will be surprised at the total dollars spent on small things as compared to the large purchases. Include in this amount the wasted interest and needless bank charges that show up on your bank statements. Treat these little expenditures very seriously.

A Note on Technology

Some of you are very savvy with electronic payments and paperless statements. You can simply tap your card for multiple purchases of less then one hundred dollars. There are also apps that you can get for your phone to track your spending. These can be good and I applaud your knowledge of these things. But studies have shown that writing on paper is the most effective way of retaining information. I don't believe getting a list of these small expenditures on your phone at the end of the month is as effective. I think the spiral notebook is the best way to go.

Take Charge

Go out today and buy two little spiral notebooks and get into the habit of recording every penny spent.

Chapter 13

Don't Budget

What About A Budget?

Many financial experts and TV know-it-alls claim that you must have a budget. They want you to plan your spending. I disagree and here is why. Simply put, a budget breaks down your expected spending into many small slices. Some financial personalities go so far as to recommend that you have 8-10 separate jars and at the beginning of the month you put the budgeted amount for each of the categories in cash into their separate jar. This, in essence, is the amount you can spend for that category. The theory is that if you underestimate and do not have enough cash in one of the jars, you do without until the end of the month.

If this happens to the grocery or car expense jar you know it is impossible to do without so we both know that you will borrow from your savings or your emergency account to make up the shortfall. It is just not a practical way to get ahead.

Next month you conclude that you underestimated what you needed for the jar that ran short and you adjust your budget to fit.

The real danger is that if, for example, you have money still left in the eating out jar at the end of the month, you think you can splurge on a nice restaurant meal and use up the surplus. Of course, you do not have to eat out, but human nature being what it is, we feel that we have this money on hand, which is allocated for eating out, so we should use it up.

We know that governments and school boards do this all the time. They are so used to budgets having surpluses in one area that they have a policy of use it or lose it. They even plan to run deficits and spend way more money than they have. But this option is not available to you or me. In my humble opinion it is much simpler and more accurate to follow the spiral notebook plan and keep every department under control. It really becomes valuable if on your date night, you strive to have some left over. You then put this into your emergency account, or as I call it the Oh Crap account, and watch it grow into something substantial.

What is An "Oh Crap" Account?

Remember that time in February when you rushed out to start your car on a cold morning? You pressed the starter button and the engine went grrh, grrrh, grrrrrh. I'll bet you said Oh Crap or something worse!

You know you have to get a new battery. You have two choices:

1. Buy it and pay for it from your Oh Crap account.

2. Buy it with your credit card (worst debt) and pay the minimum amount until it is paid off.

Choice number one will give you a headache for the rest of the day. We now know that choice number two will mess up your life for years as you struggle to pay it off.

The wise thing to do is to have an emergency account so you will always have money on hand to cover these unexpected events. In real life unpleasant events will happen from time to time. If money is taken from the emergency account, replace it right away.

Warning: never, ever use the Oh Crap money for vacations, Birthday/Christmas/Wedding presents or other expenses that you knew were coming. Emergencies only.

Take Charge

If you were to take a consolidation loan to pay off your bills, you will usually have a month before the first payment is due. Take the money you would normally be using to pay your bills and set up your Oh Crap account. Keep adding to it until you have more than enough to cover any unexpected expenses.

Chapter 14

Offers And Tricks To Avoid

A Word Of Caution About Rewards

In my opinion, most people should not choose a card that offers travel rewards. These cards encourage you to travel – naturally. Notice all the advertising about these cards. You will see that they entice you to take exotic vacations to exotic locations. Of course you will have to spend a lot of extra money while on these "free vacations." You will put this extra spending on your credit card. Guess what? For the privilege of spending in a foreign currency, the bank will charge you an extra 2-½% on every purchase you make! These travel cards will put you further into the hole.

Instead, choose a no-fee card that gives you cash back. Then you can use that money any way you want and not get sucked further into debt. You never will see your points "disappear", as recently happened with Air Miles. The card company cannot arbitrarily increase the number of points needed for your trip, as has happened with Aeroplan. You are far better off getting cash back once a year. Cash is always cash, and you can use it when and where you choose.

Remember, "You are NOT richer than you think." That is a lie. He with the gold makes the rule. He also makes the advertisement.

Retirement Saving and College Saving Plans

I have to tread softly here because I have little or no experience with these but remember they are promoted by the banks and by brokers who want to make money off you. Some people invest in RRSPs because the banks say it is a good thing but remember they make money off of you.

The big allure with an RRSP is that you do not have to initially pay tax of 40-50% on the money you put aside. The kicker is that you will have to pay tax any time you take out the money for an emergency, and when you do, it will push your rate that year into a higher tax bracket. Then you will owe the taxman more. If you never take cash out of an RRSP before it matures, remember that someday you will be forced to cash out and on that day the taxman always comes first. These plans are NOT tax exempt. I have had people brag that they have $100,000 in an RRSP. The fact is that if and when they went to use that money, they will find that they really only have $60,000. The rest vanished in taxes.

In my opinion it is cheaper to pay your taxes today. When we look at the huge and rising deficits in Canada and especially Ontario, I can guarantee you will be paying even higher tax rates when you retire than what you are paying today so why not get it over with now?

If you use an RRSP, you will be lucky to get a 5% return on your money. From this 5% you will then have to pay the bank 1 1/2% fee for their work managing the fund and eventually you must pay tax before you get to use your money. Your best-case scenario is a return of 3-½% minus the required tax. Remember, it is also possible that you might lose money in an RRSP if the stock market falls.

Here is a far better idea. If you have extra money, pay off your 20% interest credit card and your 3-4% mortgage. If you do this, you will always win and it is impossible to lose a penny regardless if the stock market goes up or down and there is no tax on the money you save.

To put it simply, the banks would like you to pay them 20% interest on your debt while they are encouraging you to accept a maybe 3½% from them in your RRSP. That seems unfair to me.

You will be way ahead if you get rid of all your debt before you even think about an RRSP. The only exception to this rule is when a company forces you to contribute and/or also makes a matching contribution to your plan. In this case, it may be OK.

The same rules apply to College Saving Plans – they are just another way for the banks to get your money.

After you are totally free of all debt on which you are paying interest, then it is time to consider investing in an RRSP. All the advertising promoting must be looked at wisely and remember the bad Golden Rule.

Chapter 15

To Do List

What You Have To Do

Well, there you have my two cents worth. I have a passion to see you get ahead and get free from the bondage of debt. I hope that you have caught my passion. I have put my thoughts, experience and knowledge into this little book and now you must do a few things for yourself.

1. Don't spend a penny unless you already have at least that amount saved.

2. Immediately buy two spiral notebooks so you and your spouse or friend can keep track of every penny spent. Plan now for your date night.

3. If you are not using a credit card, return it to the credit card company requesting that they cancel the card and ask them to notify the credit agency.

4. Write to all your credit card companies and request (or demand) that they put you on an automatic payment plan. Make sure they take the balance down to zero every month.

5. Cancel any credit card that gives travel rewards. Cancel in writing.

6. Apply for a no-fee credit card that gives cash back.

7. As soon as your credit payment history improves, request that the credit card company increase your limit. Pick a figure two to five times more than your current limit.

8. Open an Oh Crap Account. You can slowly build up the amount until you have sufficient funds to cover any emergency.

9. Put the money you are now saving through not paying interest into a special account and pay down your mortgage whenever you can do so without paying a penalty.

10. Stop paying into an RRSP and put this money into your mortgage pay down account.

Chapter 16

Wrapping It All Up

Summary

I am sure that you, like everybody else who has read this far, would like to be better off and richer by a quarter of a million dollars. That is a lot of money and I guarantee that you will be if you follow the steps outlined in this booklet. There is only one catch.

Your situation will not get any better until you begin taking the steps suggested. Some can be taken right away and some will have to be done later. Examine the list above and determine which are the "right away" things that can be done now. Take those steps and do them right now. At that point you will have begun your journey to financial freedom.

You will have noticed that none of the suggestions outlined in this book involved two jobs, job changes or working harder or working longer. You can mostly live the same lifestyle but you must live smarter. You must keep your eye on your beacon and perhaps delay some purchases or pleasures until you actually have the money. Believe me, it is worth the very small sacrifice.

Even if you fall down, recover quickly and get back in the saddle. Of course, some people will procrastinate and never get around to improving their situation, but I hope that is not you. It is a long-term goal and it will take half a lifetime to achieve, but the freedom is worth the sacrifices you are called upon to do today.

The following chapter contains some new facts, which should encourage you even more to take the first step.

Chapter 17

But Wait! There's More!

In my passion, I have tried to show you just how serious and expensive it is to overlook and ignore the warnings about having the worst kind of debt. To get your attention, I began the book with a goofy story about comparing Mr. & Mrs. Contented with Mr. & Mrs. Frustrated. I claimed that they had exactly the same lifestyle but that the Contenteds would have saved a quarter of a million dollars in interest payments. That statement was wrong.

I only said this to get your attention.

The actual amount is much, much *higher*, and I can prove it! The problem is, I'm afraid if I had said a difference of $550,000.00 you would have written me off as a crackpot and read no further. I hope that after reading this little book, I have developed some credibility with you and you will not dismiss all I have said.

The real mathematical difference between the two couples actually is $550,000 at today's low interest rates. If, and when rates increase, the difference will be even greater.

My calculations are based upon the Contenteds having a mortgage of $400,000, who pay off their credit card debt at the end of each month. The Frustrateds also have a mortgage of $400,000 and have accumulated $40,000. in credit card debt. They only pay the minimum monthly payment.

Because of their daily living habits Mr. & Mrs. Contented have a beacon score of 790 and Mr. & Mrs. Frustrated have a beacon of 485.

At the end of 30 years both couples will have paid off their mortgages. The Contenteds have never carried any credit card debt past the due date but the Frustrateds still owe their balance of $40,000.

Mr. & Mrs. Frustrated will have paid $433,104 interest on their mortgage at 6.9% and $240,000 interest on their credit card for a total of $673,104. They still owe $40,000 on their credit cards.

Mr. & Mrs. Contented will have paid $122,734 interest on their mortgage at 2.25% and zero interest on their credit card.

The real difference in the two lifestyles is $550,370 or over half of a million dollars in 30 years! It is just simple math and having an understanding of how the system works.

The only difference in the two couples is their habit of paying off their credit cards and the beacon score they have earned.

Now, I hope you see how important it is to: "*Always, always, keep your eye on the beacon.*"

After reading this booklet, I hope you believe all I have said and you will take these simple steps to become totally debt and burden free.

Remember God wants to bless you.